Hours & Wage

Record Book

Employer Name/ Company Name	Employee Name	Date of Birth

Week ending	1st	2nd	3rd	4th	5th	6th	7th	Total hours	Rate	allowances

Employee address	Class of work	
	F/time, P/time Casual, Temp	

Gross wage	Tax	Net pay	contribution plan	Signature

Employer Name/ Company Name	Employee Name	Date of Birth

Week ending	1st	2nd	3rd	4th	5th	6th	7th	Total hours	Rate	allowances

Employee address	Class of work	
	F/time, P/time Casual, Temp	

Gross wage	Tax	Net pay	contribution plan	Signature

Employer Name/ Company Name	Employee Name	Date of Birth

Week ending	1st	2nd	3rd	4th	5th	6th	7th	Total hours	Rate	allowances

Employee address	Class of work	
	F/time, P/time Casual, Temp	

Gross wage	Tax	Net pay	contribution plan	Signature

Employer Name/ Company Name	Employee Name	Date of Birth

Week ending	1st	2nd	3rd	4th	5th	6th	7th	Total hours	Rate	allowances

Employee address	Class of work	
	F/time, P/time Casual, Temp	

Gross wage	Tax	Net pay	contribution plan	Signature

Employer Name/ Company Name	Employee Name	Date of Birth

Week ending	1st	2nd	3rd	4th	5th	6th	7th	Total hours	Rate	allowances

Employee address	Class of work	
	F/time, P/time Casual, Temp	

Gross wage	Tax	Net pay	contribution plan	Signature

Employer Name/ Company Name	Employee Name	Date of Birth

Week ending	1st	2nd	3rd	4th	5th	6th	7th	Total hours	Rate	allowances

Employee address	Class of work	
	F/time, P/time Casual, Temp	

Gross wage	Tax	Net pay	contribution plan	Signature

Employer Name/ Company Name	Employee Name	Date of Birth

Week ending	1st	2nd	3rd	4th	5th	6th	7th	Total hours	Rate	allowances

Employee address	Class of work	
	F/time, P/time Casual, Temp	

Gross wage	Tax	Net pay	contribution plan	Signature

Employer Name/ Company Name	Employee Name	Date of Birth

Week ending	1st	2nd	3rd	4th	5th	6th	7th	Total hours	Rate	allowances

Employee address	Class of work	
	F/time, P/time Casual, Temp	

Gross wage	Tax	Net pay	contribution plan	Signature

Employer Name/ Company Name	Employee Name	Date of Birth

Week ending	1st	2nd	3rd	4th	5th	6th	7th	Total hours	Rate	allowances

Employee address	Class of work	
	F/time, P/time Casual, Temp	

Gross wage	Tax	Net pay	contribution plan	Signature

Employer Name/ Company Name	Employee Name	Date of Birth

Week ending	1st	2nd	3rd	4th	5th	6th	7th	Total hours	Rate	allowances

Employee address	Class of work	
	F/time, P/time Casual, Temp	

Gross wage	Tax	Net pay	contribution plan	Signature

Employer Name/ Company Name	Employee Name	Date of Birth

Week ending	1st	2nd	3rd	4th	5th	6th	7th	Total hours	Rate	allowances

Employee address	Class of work	
	F/time, P/time Casual, Temp	

Gross wage	Tax	Net pay	contribution plan	Signature

Employer Name/ Company Name	Employee Name	Date of Birth

Week ending	1st	2nd	3rd	4th	5th	6th	7th	Total hours	Rate	allowances

Employee address	Class of work	
	F/time, P/time Casual, Temp	

Gross wage	Tax	Net pay	contribution plan	Signature

Employer Name/ Company Name	Employee Name	Date of Birth

Week ending	1st	2nd	3rd	4th	5th	6th	7th	Total hours	Rate	allowances

Employee address	Class of work	
	F/time, P/time Casual, Temp	

Gross wage	Tax	Net pay	contribution plan	Signature

Employer Name/ Company Name	Employee Name	Date of Birth

Week ending	1st	2nd	3rd	4th	5th	6th	7th	Total hours	Rate	allowances

Employee address	Class of work	
	F/time, P/time Casual, Temp	

Gross wage	Tax	Net pay	contribution plan	Signature

Employer Name/ Company Name	Employee Name	Date of Birth

Week ending	1st	2nd	3rd	4th	5th	6th	7th	Total hours	Rate	allowances

Employee address	Class of work	
	F/time, P/time Casual, Temp	

Gross wage	Tax	Net pay	contribution plan	Signature

Employer Name/ Company Name	Employee Name	Date of Birth

Week ending	1st	2nd	3rd	4th	5th	6th	7th	Total hours	Rate	allowances

Employee address	Class of work	
	F/time, P/time Casual, Temp	

Gross wage	Tax	Net pay	contribution plan	Signature

Employer Name/ Company Name	Employee Name	Date of Birth

Week ending	1st	2nd	3rd	4th	5th	6th	7th	Total hours	Rate	allowances

Employee address	Class of work	
	F/time, P/time Casual, Temp	

Gross wage	Tax	Net pay	contribution plan	Signature

Employer Name/ Company Name	Employee Name	Date of Birth

Week ending	1st	2nd	3rd	4th	5th	6th	7th	Total hours	Rate	allowances

Employee address	Class of work	
	F/time, P/time Casual, Temp	

Gross wage	Tax	Net pay	contribution plan	Signature

Employer Name/ Company Name	Employee Name	Date of Birth

Week ending	1st	2nd	3rd	4th	5th	6th	7th	Total hours	Rate	allowances

Employee address	Class of work	
	F/time, P/time Casual, Temp	

Gross wage	Tax	Net pay	contribution plan	Signature

Employer Name/ Company Name	Employee Name	Date of Birth

Week ending	1st	2nd	3rd	4th	5th	6th	7th	Total hours	Rate	allowances

Employee address	Class of work	
	F/time, P/time Casual, Temp	

Gross wage	Tax	Net pay	contribution plan	Signature

Employer Name/ Company Name	Employee Name	Date of Birth

Week ending	1st	2nd	3rd	4th	5th	6th	7th	Total hours	Rate	allowances

Employee address	Class of work	
	F/time, P/time Casual, Temp	

Gross wage	Tax	Net pay	contribution plan	Signature

Employer Name/ Company Name	Employee Name	Date of Birth

Week ending	1st	2nd	3rd	4th	5th	6th	7th	Total hours	Rate	allowances

Employee address	Class of work	
	F/time, P/time Casual, Temp	

Gross wage	Tax	Net pay	contribution plan	Signature

Employer Name/ Company Name	Employee Name	Date of Birth

Week ending	1st	2nd	3rd	4th	5th	6th	7th	Total hours	Rate	allowances

Employee address	Class of work	
	F/time, P/time Casual, Temp	

Gross wage	Tax	Net pay	contribution plan	Signature

Employer Name/ Company Name	Employee Name	Date of Birth

Week ending	1st	2nd	3rd	4th	5th	6th	7th	Total hours	Rate	allowances

Employee address	Class of work	
	F/time, P/time Casual, Temp	

Gross wage	Tax	Net pay	contribution plan	Signature

Employer Name/ Company Name	Employee Name	Date of Birth

Week ending	1st	2nd	3rd	4th	5th	6th	7th	Total hours	Rate	allowances

Employee address	Class of work	
	F/time, P/time Casual, Temp	

Gross wage	Tax	Net pay	contribution plan	Signature

Employer Name/ Company Name	Employee Name	Date of Birth

Week ending	1st	2nd	3rd	4th	5th	6th	7th	Total hours	Rate	allowances

Employee address	Class of work	
	F/time, P/time Casual, Temp	

Gross wage	Tax	Net pay	contribution plan	Signature

Employer Name/ Company Name	Employee Name	Date of Birth

Week ending	1st	2nd	3rd	4th	5th	6th	7th	Total hours	Rate	allowances

Employee address	Class of work	
	F/time, P/time Casual, Temp	

Gross wage	Tax	Net pay	contribution plan	Signature

Employer Name/ Company Name	Employee Name	Date of Birth

Week ending	1st	2nd	3rd	4th	5th	6th	7th	Total hours	Rate	allowances

Employee address	Class of work	
	F/time, P/time Casual, Temp	

Gross wage	Tax	Net pay	contribution plan	Signature

Employer Name/ Company Name	Employee Name	Date of Birth

Week ending	1st	2nd	3rd	4th	5th	6th	7th	Total hours	Rate	allowances

Employee address	Class of work	
	F/time, P/time Casual, Temp	

Gross wage	Tax	Net pay	contribution plan	Signature

Employer Name/ Company Name	Employee Name	Date of Birth

Week ending	1st	2nd	3rd	4th	5th	6th	7th	Total hours	Rate	allowances

Employee address	Class of work	
	F/time, P/time Casual, Temp	

Gross wage	Tax	Net pay	contribution plan	Signature

Employer Name/ Company Name	Employee Name	Date of Birth

Week ending	1st	2nd	3rd	4th	5th	6th	7th	Total hours	Rate	allowances

Employee address	Class of work	
	F/time, P/time Casual, Temp	

Gross wage	Tax	Net pay	contribution plan	Signature

Employer Name/ Company Name	Employee Name	Date of Birth

Week ending	1st	2nd	3rd	4th	5th	6th	7th	Total hours	Rate	allowances

Employee address	Class of work	
	F/time, P/time Casual, Temp	

Gross wage	Tax	Net pay	contribution plan	Signature

Employer Name/ Company Name	Employee Name	Date of Birth

Week ending	1st	2nd	3rd	4th	5th	6th	7th	Total hours	Rate	allowances

Employee address	Class of work	
	F/time, P/time Casual, Temp	

Gross wage	Tax	Net pay	contribution plan	Signature

Employer Name/ Company Name	Employee Name	Date of Birth

Week ending	1st	2nd	3rd	4th	5th	6th	7th	Total hours	Rate	allowance

Employee address	Class of work	
	F/time, P/time Casual, Temp	

Gross wage	Tax	Net pay	contribution plan	Signature

Employer Name/ Company Name	Employee Name	Date of Birth

Week ending	1st	2nd	3rd	4th	5th	6th	7th	Total hours	Rate	allowances

Employee address	Class of work	
	F/time, P/time Casual, Temp	

Gross wage	Tax	Net pay	contribution plan	Signature

Employer Name/ Company Name	Employee Name	Date of Birth

Week ending	1st	2nd	3rd	4th	5th	6th	7th	Total hours	Rate	allowances

Employee address	Class of work	
	F/time, P/time Casual, Temp	

Gross wage	Tax	Net pay	contribution plan	Signature

Employer Name/ Company Name	Employee Name	Date of Birth

Week ending	1st	2nd	3rd	4th	5th	6th	7th	Total hours	Rate	allowances

Employee address	Class of work	
	F/time, P/time Casual, Temp	

Gross wage	Tax	Net pay	contribution plan	Signature

Employer Name/ Company Name	Employee Name	Date of Birth

Week ending	1st	2nd	3rd	4th	5th	6th	7th	Total hours	Rate	allowances

Employee address	Class of work	
	F/time, P/time Casual, Temp	

Gross wage	Tax	Net pay	contribution plan	Signature

Employer Name/ Company Name	Employee Name	Date of Birth

Week ending	1st	2nd	3rd	4th	5th	6th	7th	Total hours	Rate	allowances

Employee address	Class of work	
	F/time, P/time Casual, Temp	

Gross wage	Tax	Net pay	contribution plan	Signature

Employer Name/ Company Name	Employee Name	Date of Birth

Week ending	1st	2nd	3rd	4th	5th	6th	7th	Total hours	Rate	allowances

Employee address	Class of work	
	F/time, P/time Casual, Temp	

Gross wage	Tax	Net pay	contribution plan	Signature

Employer Name/ Company Name	Employee Name	Date of Birth

Week ending	1st	2nd	3rd	4th	5th	6th	7th	Total hours	Rate	allowances

Employee address	Class of work	
	F/time, P/time Casual, Temp	

Gross wage	Tax	Net pay	contribution plan	Signature

Employer Name/ Company Name	Employee Name	Date of Birth

Week ending	1st	2nd	3rd	4th	5th	6th	7th	Total hours	Rate	allowances

Employee address	Class of work	
	F/time, P/time Casual, Temp	

Gross wage	Tax	Net pay	contribution plan	Signature

Employer Name/ Company Name	Employee Name	Date of Birth

Week ending	1st	2nd	3rd	4th	5th	6th	7th	Total hours	Rate	allowances

Employee address	Class of work	
	F/time, P/time Casual, Temp	

Gross wage	Tax	Net pay	contribution plan	Signature

Employer Name/ Company Name	Employee Name	Date of Birth

Week ending	1st	2nd	3rd	4th	5th	6th	7th	Total hours	Rate	allowances

Employee address	Class of work	
	F/time, P/time Casual, Temp	

Gross wage	Tax	Net pay	contribution plan	Signature

Employer Name/ Company Name	Employee Name	Date of Birth

Week ending	1st	2nd	3rd	4th	5th	6th	7th	Total hours	Rate	allowances

Employee address	Class of work	
	F/time, P/time Casual, Temp	

Gross wage	Tax	Net pay	contribution plan	Signature

Employer Name/ Company Name	Employee Name	Date of Birth

Week ending	1st	2nd	3rd	4th	5th	6th	7th	Total hours	Rate	allowance

Employee address	Class of work	
	F/time, P/time Casual, Temp	

Gross wage	Tax	Net pay	contribution plan	Signature

Employer Name/ Company Name	Employee Name	Date of Birth

Week ending	1st	2nd	3rd	4th	5th	6th	7th	Total hours	Rate	allowances

Employee address	Class of work	
	F/time, P/time Casual, Temp	

Gross wage	Tax	Net pay	contribution plan	Signature

Employer Name/ Company Name	Employee Name	Date of Birth

Week ending	1st	2nd	3rd	4th	5th	6th	7th	Total hours	Rate	allowances

Employee address	Class of work	
	F/time, P/time Casual, Temp	

Gross wage	Tax	Net pay	contribution plan	Signature

Employer Name/ Company Name	Employee Name	Date of Birth

Week ending	1st	2nd	3rd	4th	5th	6th	7th	Total hours	Rate	allowances

Employee address	Class of work	
	F/time, P/time Casual, Temp	

Gross wage	Tax	Net pay	contribution plan	Signature

Employer Name/ Company Name	Employee Name	Date of Birth

Week ending	1st	2nd	3rd	4th	5th	6th	7th	Total hours	Rate	allowances

Employee address	Class of work	
	F/time, P/time Casual, Temp	

Gross wage	Tax	Net pay	contribution plan	Signature

Employer Name/ Company Name	Employee Name	Date of Birth

Week ending	1st	2nd	3rd	4th	5th	6th	7th	Total hours	Rate	allowances

Employee address	Class of work	
	F/time, P/time Casual, Temp	

Gross wage	Tax	Net pay	contribution plan	Signature

Employer Name/ Company Name	Employee Name	Date of Birth

Week ending	1st	2nd	3rd	4th	5th	6th	7th	Total hours	Rate	allowance:

Employee address	Class of work	
	F/time, P/time Casual, Temp	

Gross wage	Tax	Net pay	contribution plan	Signature

Printed in Great Britain
by Amazon

27272778R00059